GRAPHIC LIBRARY™

W9-BQU-052

INVENTIONS AND DISCOVERY

GEORGE EASTMAN AND THE KODAK CAMERA

by Jennifer Fandel

illustrated by Gordon Purcell and Al Milgrom

Consultant:
David Silver, President
International Photographic
Historical Organization
San Francisco, California

Capstone press®

Mankato, Minnesota

Graphic Library is published by Capstone Press,
1710 Roe Crest Drive, North Mankato, Minnesota 56003.
www.capstonepub.com

Printed in the United States of America in Stevens Point, Wisconsin.
072014
008385R

Library of Congress Cataloging-in-Publication Data
Fandel, Jennifer.
George Eastman and the Kodak camera / by Jennifer Fandel; illustrated by Gordon Purcell and Al Milgrom
p. cm.—(Graphic library. Inventions and discovery)
Includes bibliographical references and index.
ISBN-13: 978-0-7368-6848-8 (hardcover)
ISBN-10: 0-7368-6848-8 (hardcover)
ISBN-13: 978-0-7368-7900-2 (softcover pbk.)
ISBN-10: 0-7368-7900-5 (softcover pbk)
1. Eastman, George, 1854-1932—Juvenile literature. 2. Photographic industry—United States—Biography—Juvenile literature. 3. Kodak camera—Juvenile literature. I. Purcell, Gordon, ill. II. Milgrom, Al, ill. III. Title. IV. Series.
TR140.E3F36 2007
770.92—dc22 [B] 2006036327

Summary: In graphic novel format, tells the story of how George Eastman developed the Kodak camera, and how his company changed the way people captured the moments of their lives.

Designer
Jason Knudson

Editor
Mandy Robbins

Colorist
Brent Schoonover

TABLE OF CONTENTS

CHAPTER 1
A HOBBY THAT CLICKED

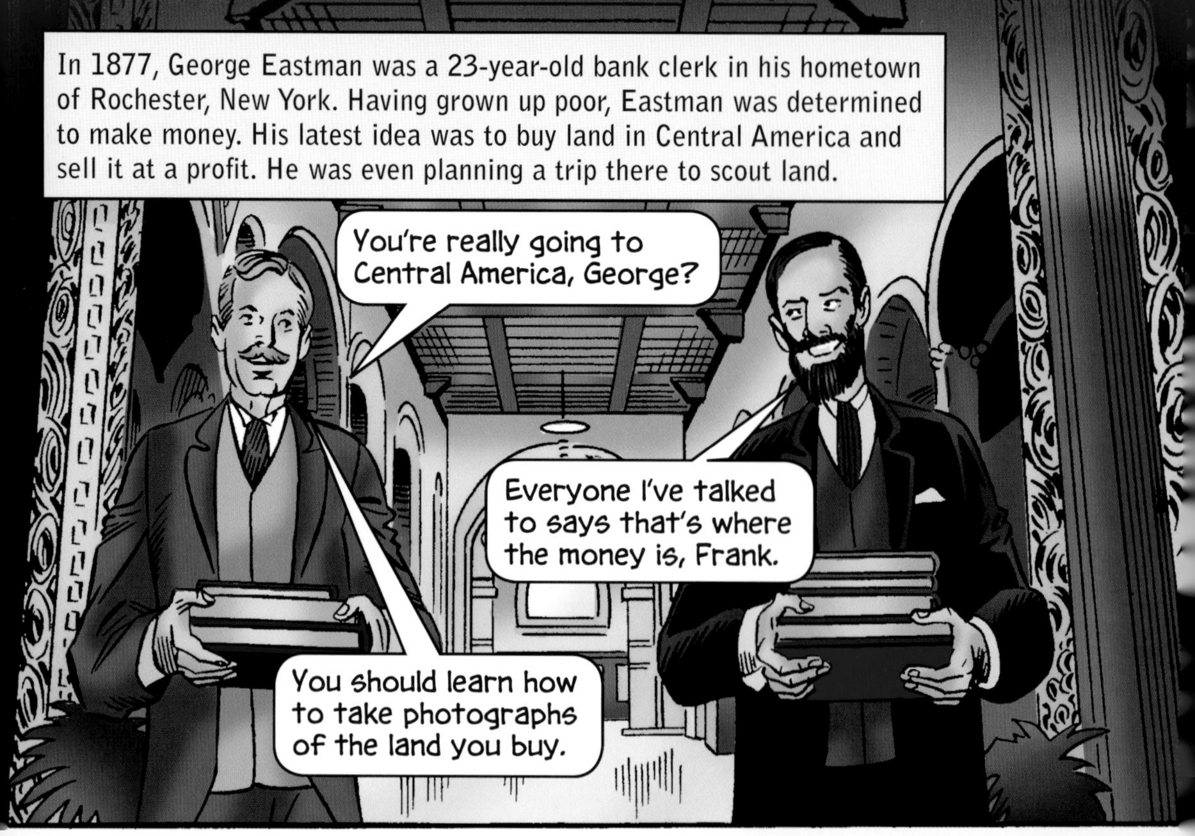
In 1877, George Eastman was a 23-year-old bank clerk in his hometown of Rochester, New York. Having grown up poor, Eastman was determined to make money. His latest idea was to buy land in Central America and sell it at a profit. He was even planning a trip there to scout land.
You're really going to Central America, George?
Everyone I've talked to says that's where the money is, Frank.
You should learn how to take photographs of the land you buy.

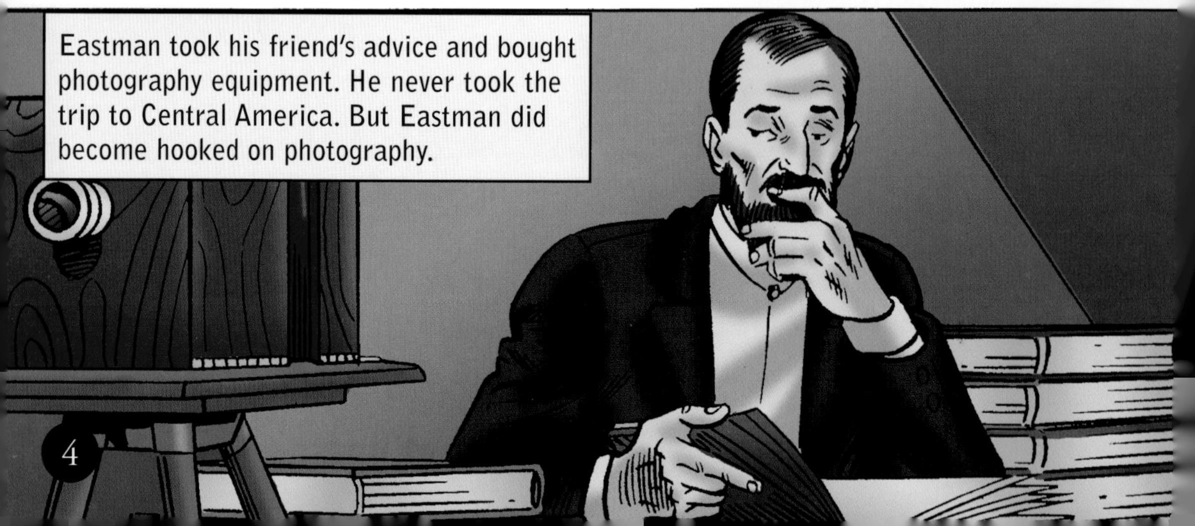
Eastman took his friend's advice and bought photography equipment. He never took the trip to Central America. But Eastman did become hooked on photography.

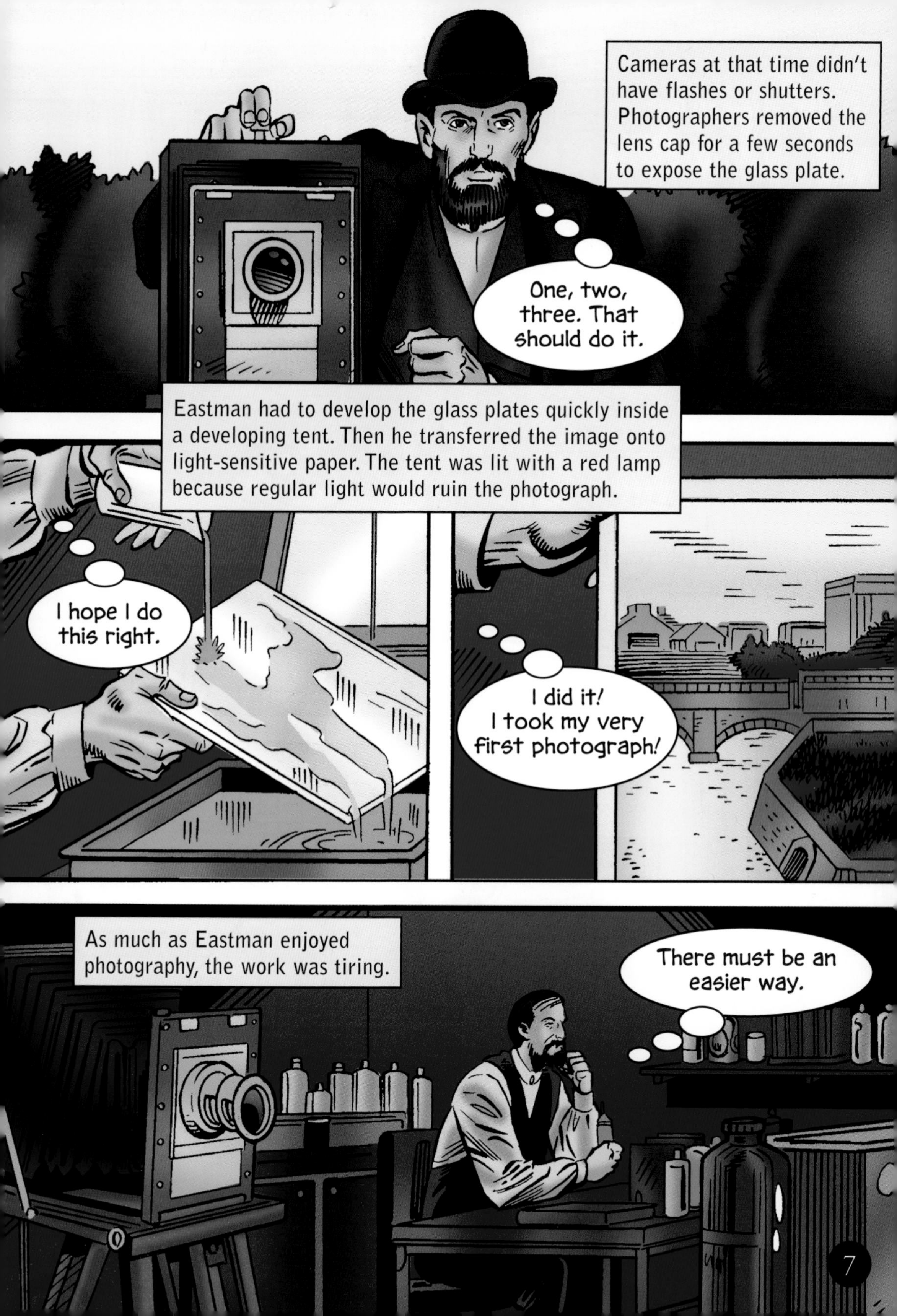

Cameras at that time didn't have flashes or shutters. Photographers removed the lens cap for a few seconds to expose the glass plate.
One, two, three. That should do it.
Eastman had to develop the glass plates quickly inside a developing tent. Then he transferred the image onto light-sensitive paper. The tent was lit with a red lamp because regular light would ruin the photograph.
I hope I do this right.
I did it! I took my very first photograph!
As much as Eastman enjoyed photography, the work was tiring.
There must be an easier way.

CHAPTER 2

A CLEAR AND SIMPLE DREAM

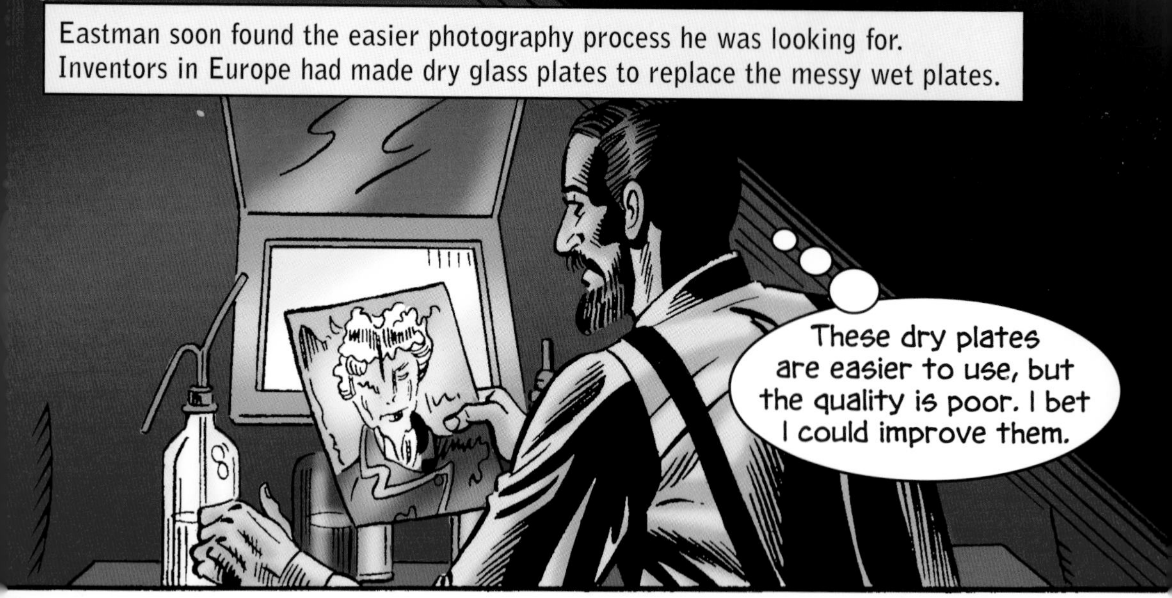
Eastman soon found the easier photography process he was looking for. Inventors in Europe had made dry glass plates to replace the messy wet plates.
These dry plates are easier to use, but the quality is poor. I bet I could improve them.

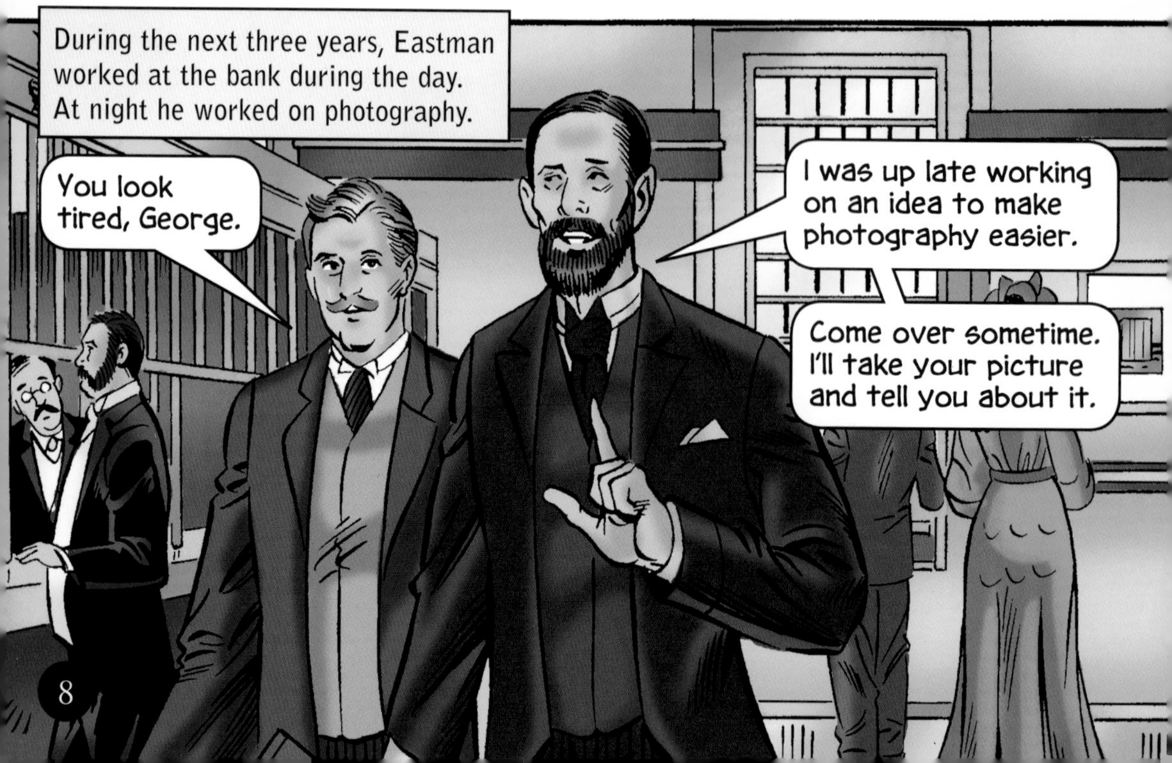
During the next three years, Eastman worked at the bank during the day. At night he worked on photography.
You look tired, George.
I was up late working on an idea to make photography easier.
Come over sometime. I'll take your picture and tell you about it.

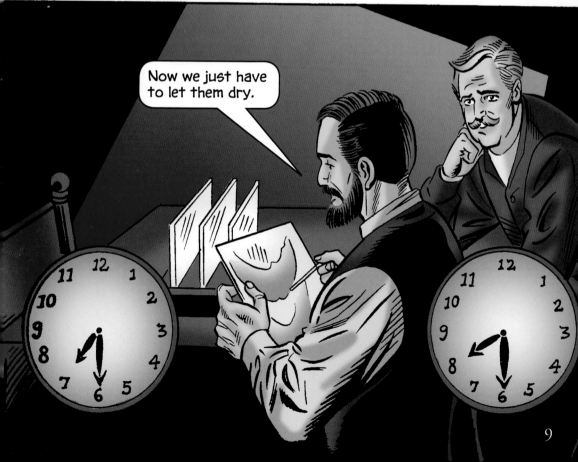

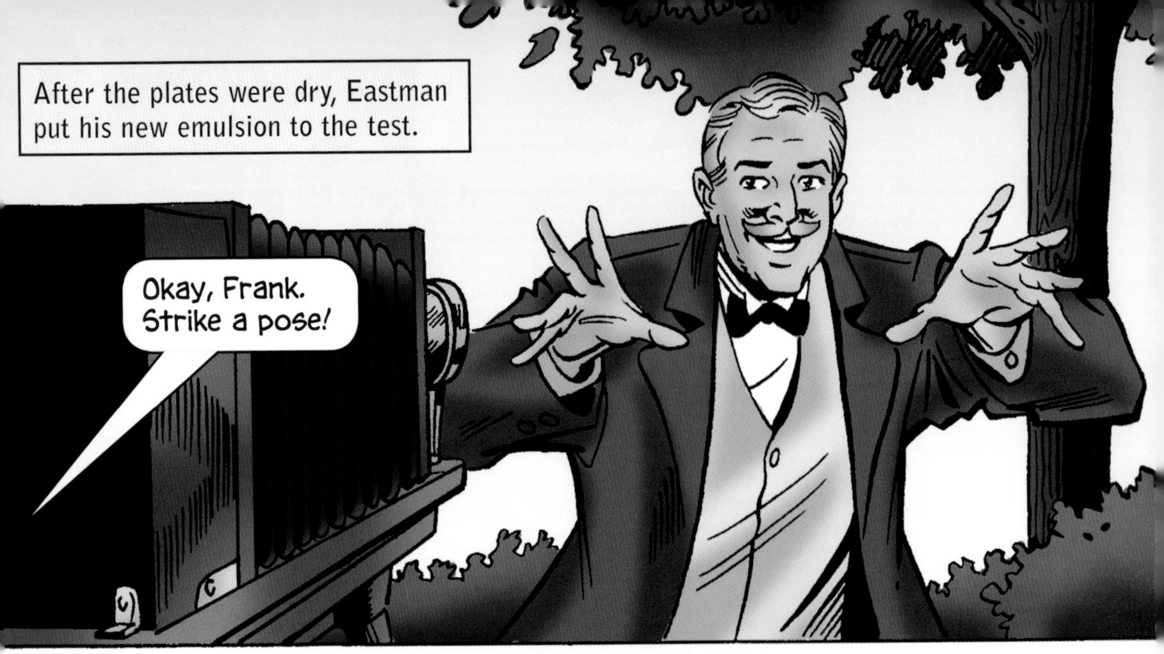
After the plates were dry, Eastman put his new emulsion to the test.
Okay, Frank. Strike a pose!

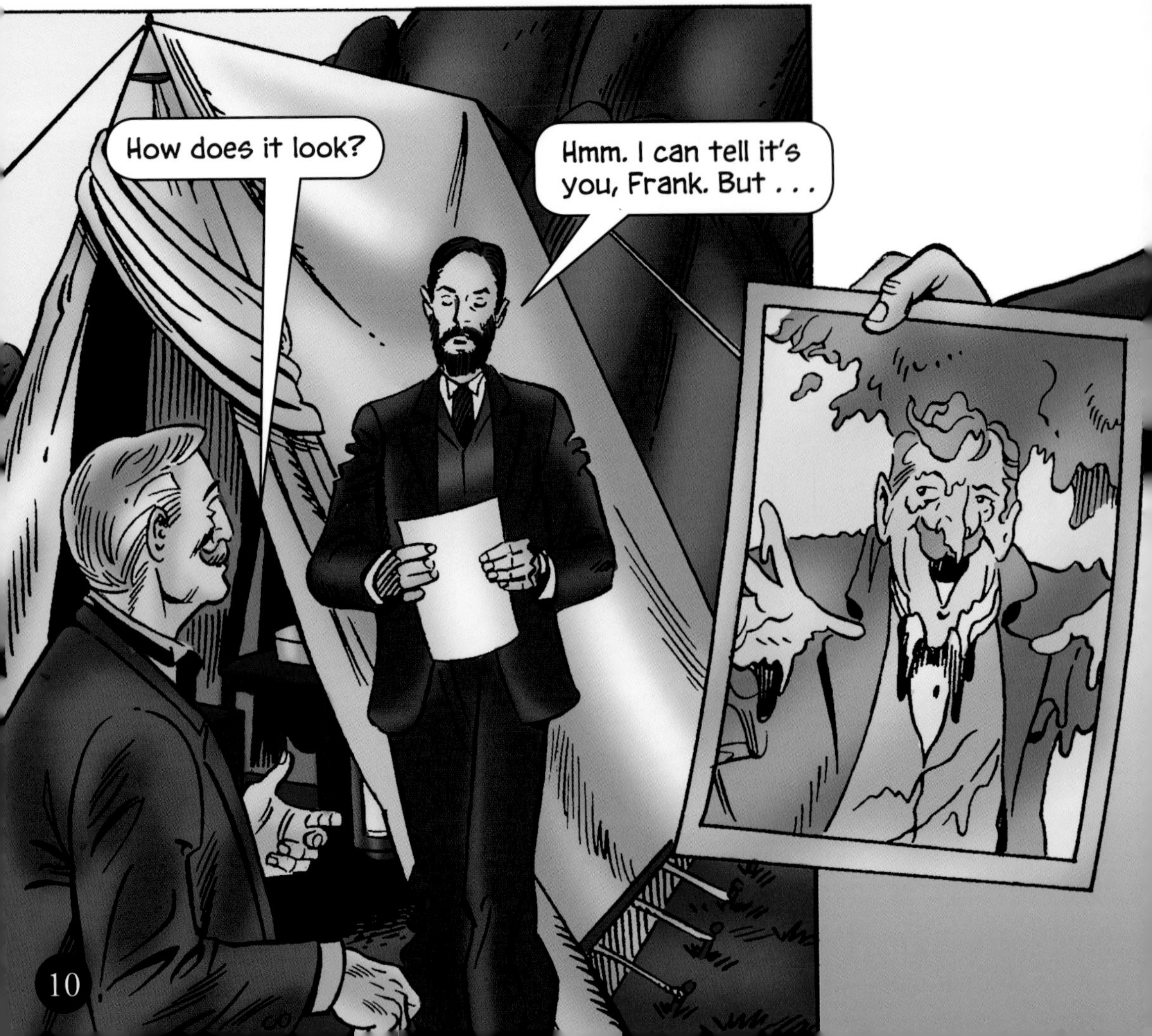
How does it look?
Hmm. I can tell it's you, Frank. But . . .

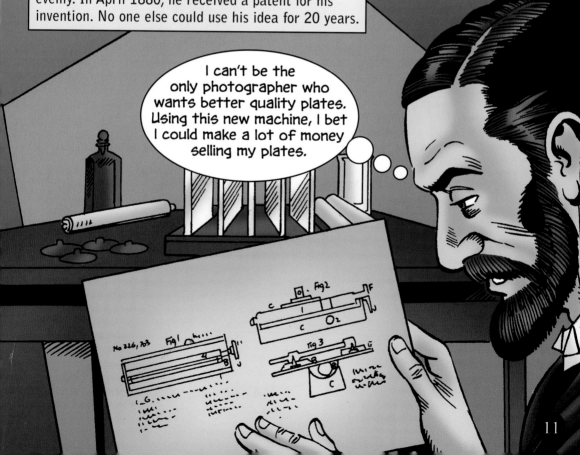

Eastman designed a machine to coat glass plates evenly. In April 1880, he received a patent for his invention. No one else could use his idea for 20 years.

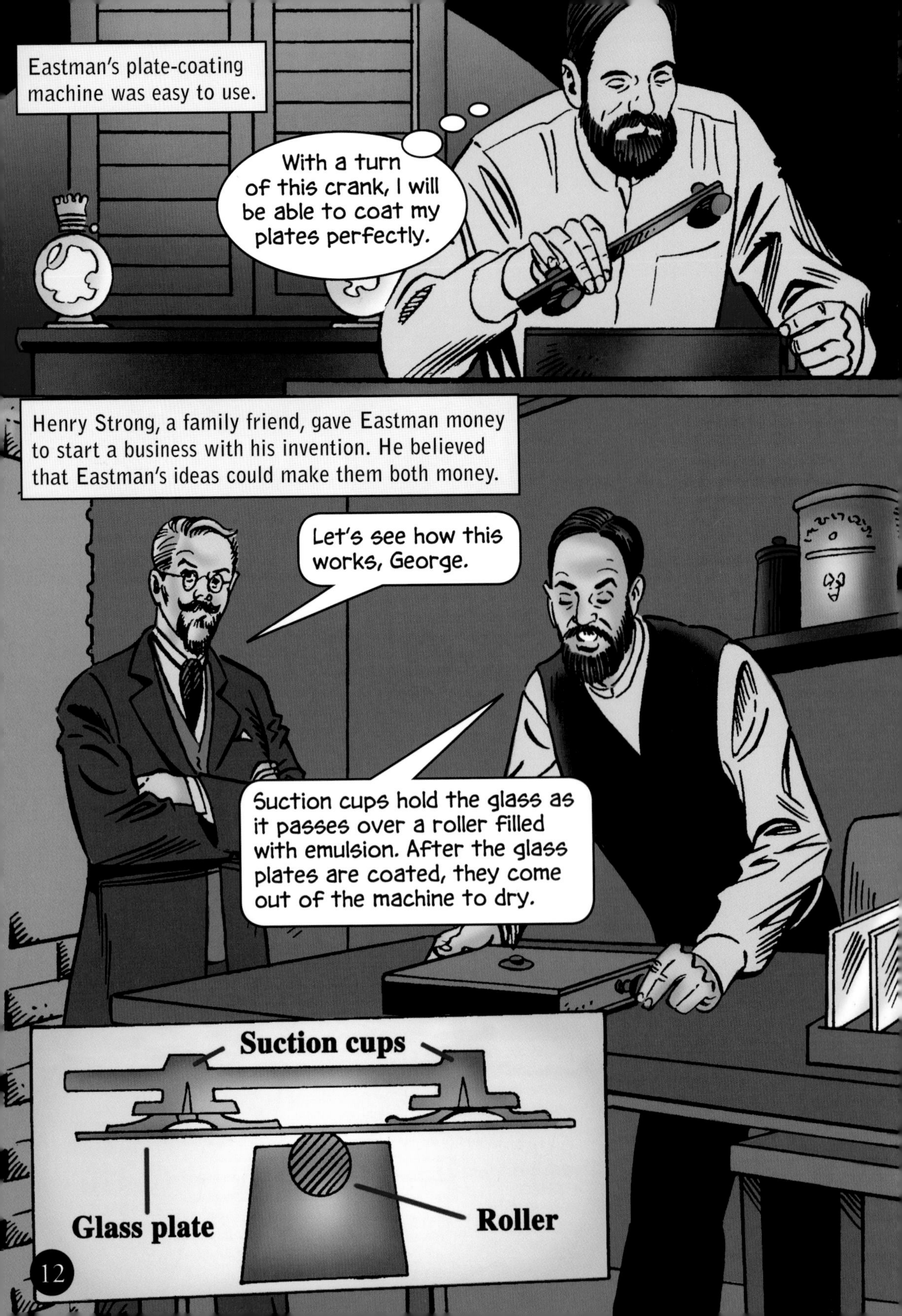
Eastman's plate-coating machine was easy to use.
With a turn of this crank, I will be able to coat my plates perfectly.
Henry Strong, a family friend, gave Eastman money to start a business with his invention. He believed that Eastman's ideas could make them both money.
Let's see how this works, George.
Suction cups hold the glass as it passes over a roller filled with emulsion. After the glass plates are coated, they come out of the machine to dry.
Suction cups
Glass plate
Roller

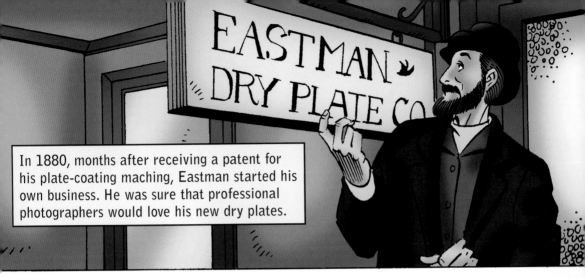

In 1880, months after receiving a patent for his plate-coating maching, Eastman started his own business. He was sure that professional photographers would love his new dry plates.

I've heard a lot about these new dry plates. How are they working?

Try them, and tell me what you think.

Eastman promised flawless plates and replaced bad ones for free. Soon, he was well-known among photographers in the United States and Europe.

Some plates had problems, but Eastman sent new ones.

I suggest his company to everyone.

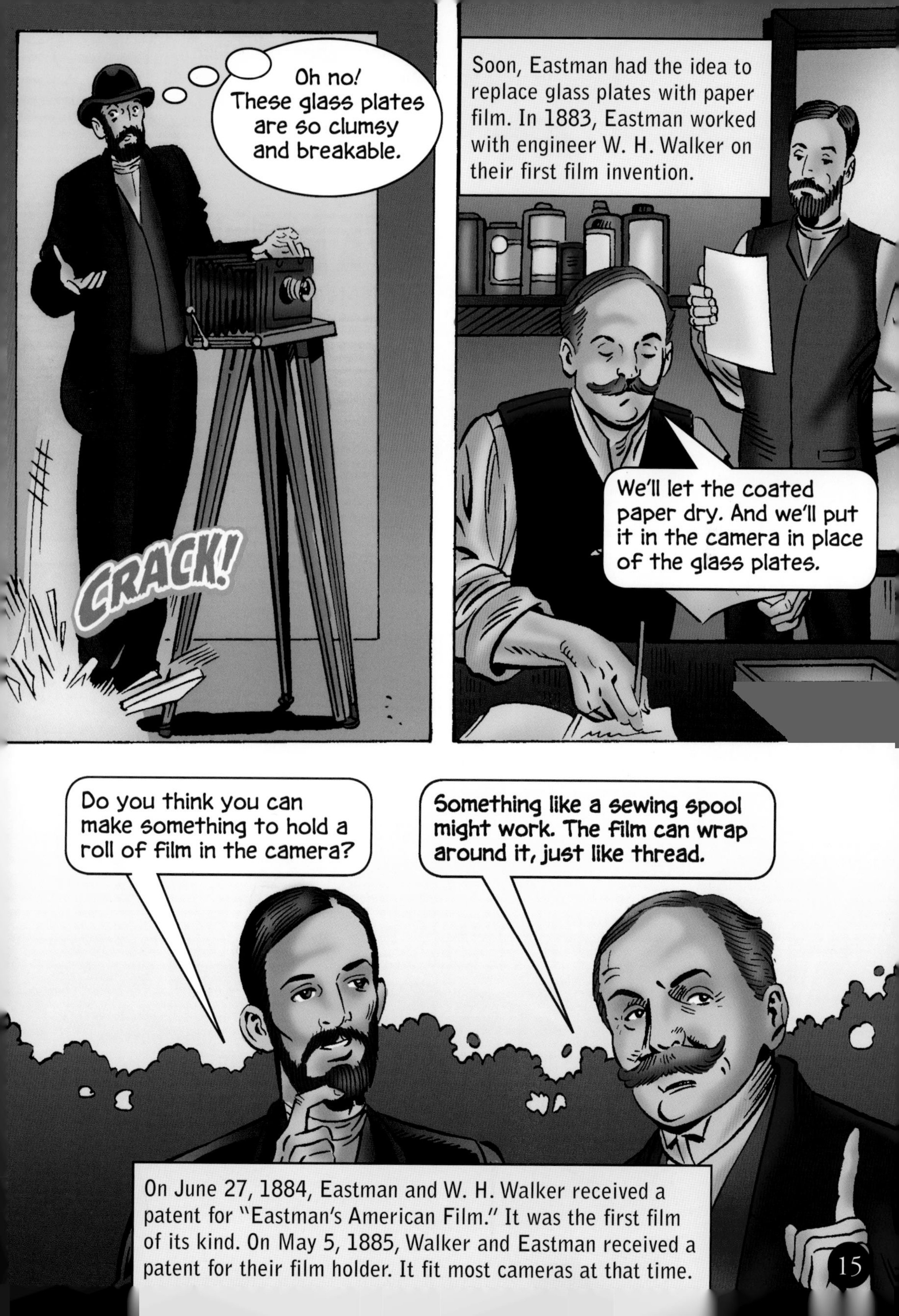
Oh no! These glass plates are so clumsy and breakable.
CRACK!
Soon, Eastman had the idea to replace glass plates with paper film. In 1883, Eastman worked with engineer W. H. Walker on their first film invention.
We'll let the coated paper dry. And we'll put it in the camera in place of the glass plates.
Do you think you can make something to hold a roll of film in the camera?
Something like a sewing spool might work. The film can wrap around it, just like thread.
On June 27, 1884, Eastman and W. H. Walker received a patent for "Eastman's American Film." It was the first film of its kind. On May 5, 1885, Walker and Eastman received a patent for their film holder. It fit most cameras at that time.

CHAPTER 3

BRINGING PHOTOGRAPHY TO THE PEOPLE

While Walker worked on making a better film, Eastman created a new type of camera. He had a cabinetmaker build the camera casing. A local machinist made a shutter that took photos quicker than other cameras. And an optical shop, owned by German immigrants named Bausch and Lomb, supplied Eastman with a camera lens.

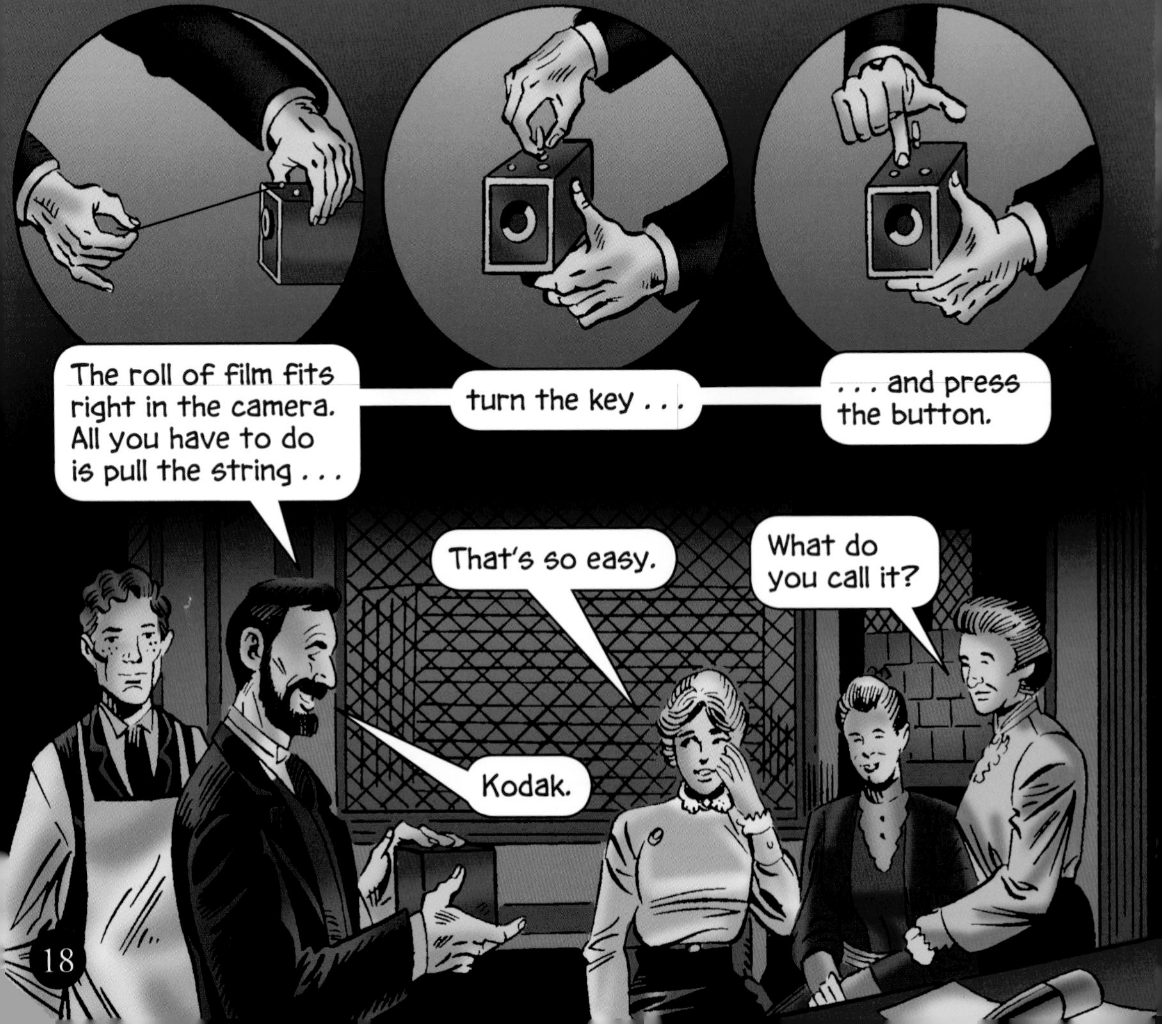

The roll of film fits right in the camera. All you have to do is pull the string . . .
turn the key . . .
. . . and press the button.
That's so easy.
What do you call it?
Kodak.

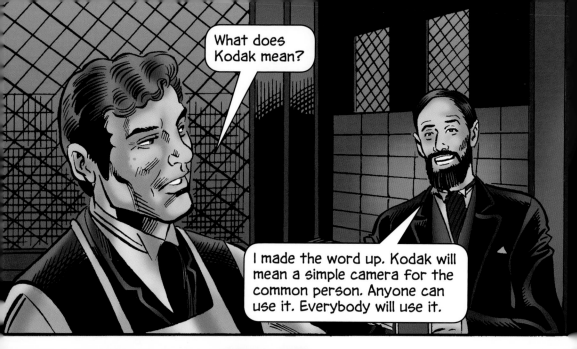

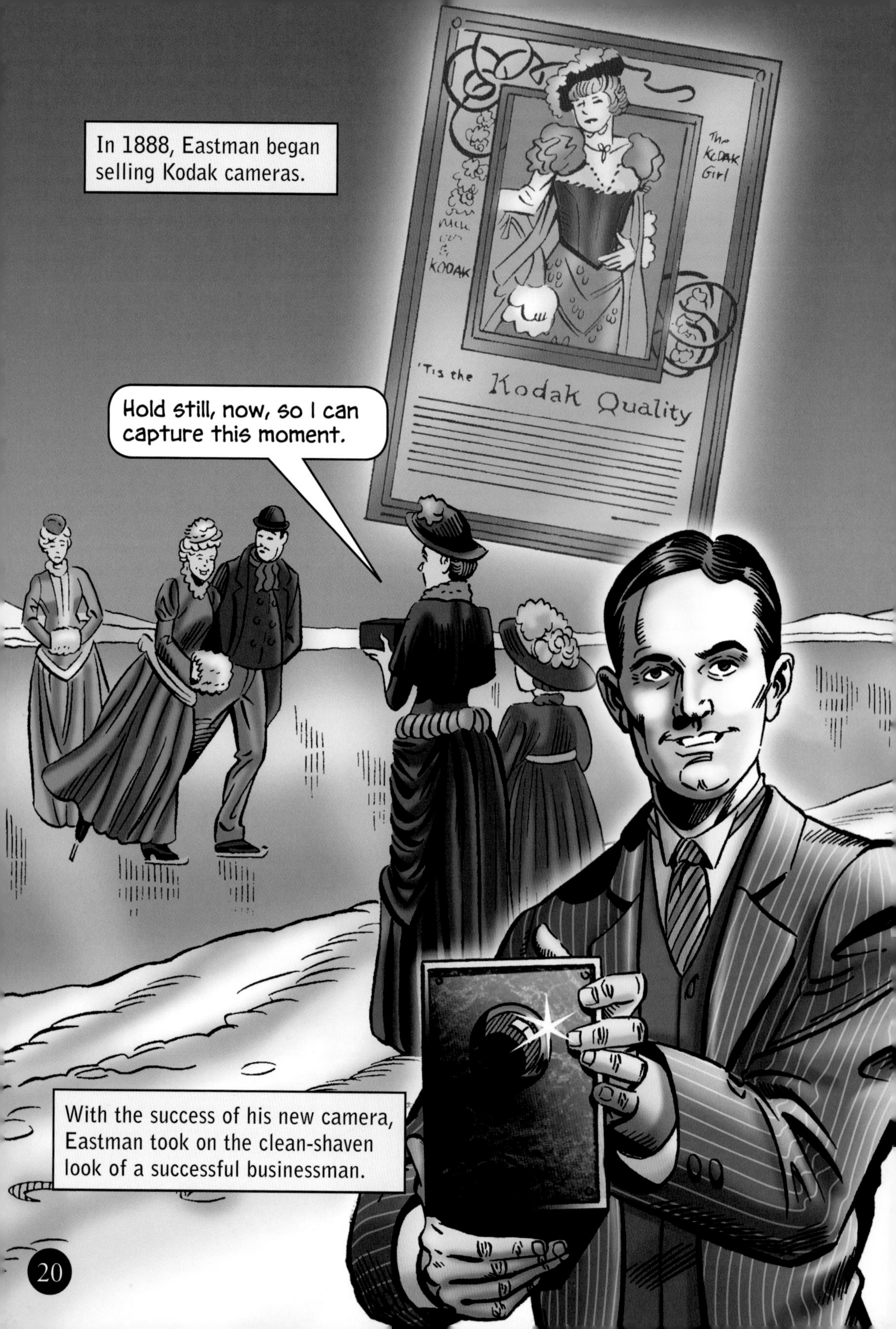
In 1888, Eastman began selling Kodak cameras.
The KODAK Girl
'Tis the Kodak Quality
Hold still, now, so I can capture this moment.
With the success of his new camera, Eastman took on the clean-shaven look of a successful businessman.

CHAPTER 4
PHOTOGRAPHY—IT'S A SNAP

For the next 10 years, Kodak cameras were in high demand. Eastman decided to expand his business. He opened factories and distribution centers around the world.

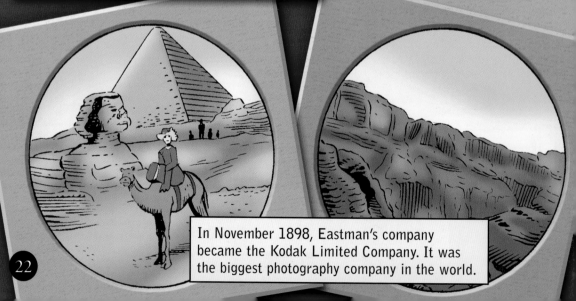

In November 1898, Eastman's company became the Kodak Limited Company. It was the biggest photography company in the world.

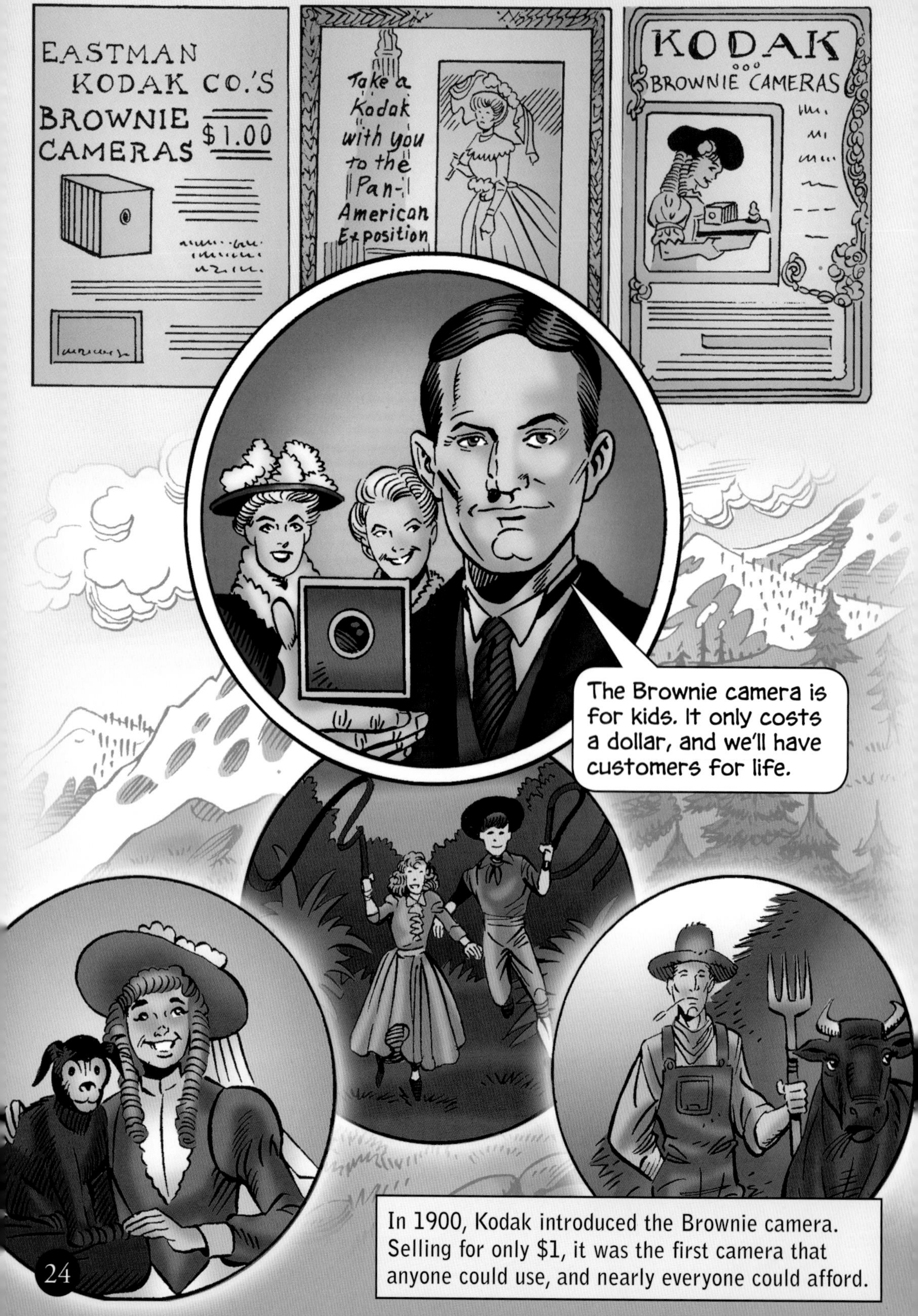
EASTMAN KODAK CO.'S BROWNIE CAMERAS $1.00
Take a Kodak with you to the Pan-American Exposition
KODAK BROWNIE CAMERAS
The Brownie camera is for kids. It only costs a dollar, and we'll have customers for life.
In 1900, Kodak introduced the Brownie camera. Selling for only $1, it was the first camera that anyone could use, and nearly everyone could afford.

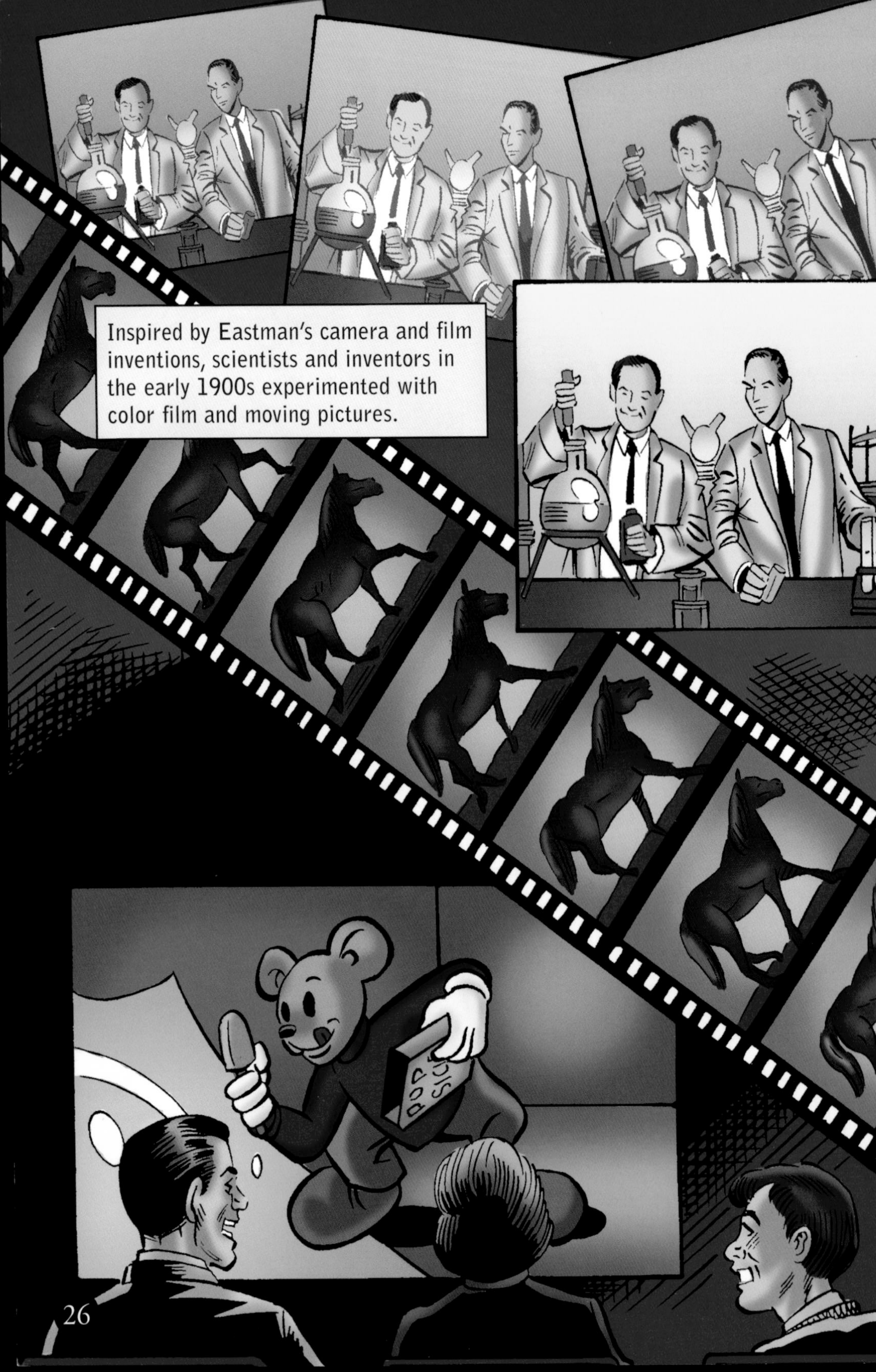
Inspired by Eastman's camera and film inventions, scientists and inventors in the early 1900s experimented with color film and moving pictures.

Photography has changed since Eastman made his first Kodak camera, but his idea has stayed the same.

Photography is quick, simple, and inexpensive, letting people capture the moments in their lives and moments in history.

George Eastman took up photography to make money. He continued in the field because he loved it.

27

MORE ABOUT
GEORGE EASTMAN
AND KODAK

⭐ George Eastman was born July 12, 1854 in a
small town outside of Rochester, New York. He died
March 14, 1932.

⭐ Eastman didn't finish high school. When his father
died, Eastman quit school at age 14 to help support
the family. He worked as an office messenger boy.

⭐ Eastman's first Kodak camera was sold for $25.
This included a roll of film for taking 100 pictures.
Customers sent their cameras to the company once
they took all their pictures. They paid $10 to have
their film developed and their camera shipped back
to them with a new roll of film.

⭐ Eastman became a millionaire, but he gave much
of his money away to universities, schools in poor
communities, and the arts.

⭐ In 1826, Frenchman Joseph Nicephore Niepce made
the first surviving photograph.